BURIED

To: Katie

Be free indeed!

♡

To: Katie

Be free indeed!
♡

Love ya

Buried

FREEDOM FROM THE SECRETS THAT SILENCE US

Sarita Conley

Sarita Conley

This book is a memoir. It reflects the author's present recollections of experiences over time. Some names and characteristics have been changed, some events have been compressed, and some dialogue has been recreated.

Copyright © 2023 by Sarita Conley

All rights reserved. No part of this book may be reproduced in any manner whatsoever without written permission except in the case of brief quotations embodied in critical articles and reviews.

First paperback edition June 2023

Scripture taken from the New King James Version®. Copyright © 1982 by Thomas Nelson. Used by permission. All rights reserved.

Scripture quotations marked (NLT) are taken from the *Holy Bible*, New Living Translation, copyright ©1996, 2004, 2015 by Tyndale House Foundation. Used by permission of Tyndale House Publishers, Carol Stream, Illinois 60188. All rights reserved.

Scripture quotations marked (AMP) are taken from the Amplified Bible, Copyright © 2015 by The Lockman Foundation. Used by permission.

Scripture quotations are from the ESV® Bible (The Holy Bible, English Standard Version®), copyright © 2001 by Crossway, a publishing ministry of Good News Publishers. Used by permission. All rights reserved. The ESV text may not be quoted in any publication made available to the public by a Creative Commons license. The ESV may not be translated in whole or in part into any other language.

OED Online. Oxford University Press, March 2023. Web. 20 June 2023

Unless otherwise specified, all definitions are from Merriam - https://www.merriam-webster.com/ (2023)

Any Internet addresses (websites, blogs, etc) in this book are offered as a resource. They are not intended in any way to be or imply any endorsements by Sarita Conley, nor does Sarita Conley vouch for the content of these sites for the life of this book. All rights reserved.

ISBN 979-8-8504-2996-6
ISBN 978-1-0881-3621-8

This book is dedicated to my God. Thank You for doing the impossible in me.

Contents

Dedication		v
Recommendation		ix
Acknowledgments		xi
Foreword		xv
Introduction		xvii
1	Shame	1
2	Self-Harm	6
3	Identity	12
4	I Kissed a Girl, and I Liked It	22
5	Situation-ships	39
6	It Doesn't Take All That	42
7	The Fall	49
8	My Little Ones	59
9	Purposeful Pits	63
10	No More Shame	68
11	Tools to Grow Your Spiritual Walk	74

12 Final Acknowledgment 77

13 Book Resources 78

Recommendation

In "Buried: Freedom from the Secrets that Silence Us," Author Sarita Conley takes us on the beautiful, sometimes painful, but very necessary journey of facing our own hidden truths in order to attain the freedom God's Word promises His believers is available. Her story is a true testimony of how God's love and deliverance power can take one from the deepest and darkest pits of shame, and lift them to a place of wholeness, holiness, and liberty. "Buried" is an amazing guide to uncovering and unveiling the secrets that are preventing us from experiencing God's transformation power because of our fear of honest confession. Allow this book to convict, provoke, and compel you to face yourself, face God, and get healed to better face your future. Unmask the truths that have the power to make you free.. and be free indeed!

Prophetess and Pastor Kristy Lyles
Outpour Christian Church
Dallas, TX

Acknowledgments

To my husband, who from the onset of knowing about the assignment God gave me, encouraged me every step of the way. Thank you for prioritizing obedience to the Lord above all else. Thank you for loving me so well that I was able to write this book without distraction or confusion.

To my mother, thank you for allowing me to interview you in preparation for this assignment. I cannot thank you enough for the ways you've shown up for me time and time again. Thank you for your endless love and prayers. Thank you for never giving up on me.

To my father, thank you for the love and acceptance you've shown me over the years. When I sat across from you and told you I would be writing a book you encouraged me to let it out. Those words were just what I needed to hear to continue going forward, knowing I had your blessing.

To my dear friend Sandra, thank you for your endless encouragement, love, and prayers throughout the fulfillment of this assignment. From the moment I shared it with you, your response was joyful. Your support along the way has meant everything to me. Thank you for being in my corner, for pushing me to do everything the Lord has called me to.

To my nana, thank you for your prayers for me! Thank you for giving me my first bible as a young girl. Thank you for every godly book you've given me when you had no idea what battles I would face. I thank you for your love for me.

To my siblings, we're all different but God gave us each other for a reason. I'm thankful for each of you. Thank you all for allowing me into your lives. We may not be the closest but each of you remain in my prayers. I love each of you more than you know.

To my nieces, nephews, and godson, each of you are so unique and special in your own right. I'm beyond blessed to have been graced with your presence. Thank you for allowing me into your lives and at times allowing me to tell you about Jesus. My prayer is that each of you would know Him for yourself, because He's worth knowing.

To my little ones, thank you for being the answer to my prayers. At just the right time, the two of you came along and changed everything. I love you both and am so thankful for our time together. Leaving you two was one of the hardest things I've had to do. I know the Lord will complete the work He began in you both.

To my mentors over the years, thank you for seeing in me what I couldn't see at the time. Thank you for selflessly pouring into me, and loving me to wholeness. Nothing was done or sacrificed in vain. God saw it all.

Foreword

When are you coming out of the pit?

Most sins start as innocent as "I'm just going to try it this one time and test it out." As you experiment with it you begin to think to yourself, "I like this." After addiction takes hold, we try to embark on healing and overcoming by our lonesome. But creation can't heal properly without its creator.

When sin becomes too influential to handle, giving in does not help the issue. When intentionally deciding to course correct, you need to first acknowledge the sin for what it is. Then, affirm to the Lord who He is in your life. From there you can position things in order to properly heal. Sarita Conley provides her testimony in "Buried: Freedom from the Secrets that Silence Us" to address the sins she battled with and overcame. Sarita explains God's commission for us to overcome shame, addiction, self-harm, depression, suicidal thoughts, abortion, alcoholism, and more. This book provides restoration from many idols we've allowed to take over our lives.

How aware are you of God's love for you? He loves you so much that He decided to buy you at a high price. The temple that you live in is a dwelling that you have authority over. We're not to take advantage of this authority but to adequately use it for the glory of God.

> *"Don't you realize that your body is the temple of the Holy Spirit, who lives in you and was given to you by God? You do not belong to yourself, for God bought you at a high price. So you must honor God with your body"*
> 1 Corinthians 6:19-20 NLT

Let's begin the journey of restoration.

-Bryant Conley

Introduction

"And I, where could I take my shame? And as for you, you would be like one of the fools in Israel. Now therefore, please speak to the king; for he will not withhold me from you."
2 Samuel 13:13 NKJV

Have you ever dug a deep hole? I mean in the literal sense. Did you excavate it with your hands, or a shovel? I never have. Growing up I watched a movie where children at a camp had to dig holes all day long in the desert. I loved that movie. Though I never physically dug any holes, I'm familiar with burying things. Have you ever buried a secret? Were you able to retrieve it when you went looking for it? Or did you not go looking for it? I get that too. Why uncover what was purposely buried?

You don't normally find people at burial sites digging up graves. Some things have to stay where they were put. Maybe that only applies to bodies. Even with excavation, artifacts are dug up because they're usually of great value. We excavate to remove earth that is covering very old objects buried in the ground, in order to discover things about the past. In Psychology, I learned it can be good and beneficial to bring things to the surface. That we all have experiences or desires that are unconscious to us, hidden from our awareness. Repression is one of the ways we do this. It's when unwanted impulses or thoughts are being unconsciously pushed out of awareness. Conversely, suppression is consciously choosing not to think about thoughts/feelings. Time and time again, we see the negative effects of stuffing things down. It can be easy to think what's out of sight is out of mind, and can't harm us. But this isn't always true. Sometimes what's "out of sight, out of mind" is crippling, and harming us more than we know.

We unconsciously and consciously bury things that cause us deep pain. We see this with trauma. Trauma can be anything that our system can't handle or process. The American Psychological Association defines trauma as an emotional response to a terrible event like an accident, rape, or natural disaster. Immediately after the event, shock and denial are typical. Longer term reactions include unpredictable emotions, flashbacks, strained relationships, and even physical symptoms like headaches or nausea. SAMHSA defines trauma as an event or circumstance resulting in physical harm, emotional harm, and or life-threatening harm. The event or circumstance has lasting adverse effects on the individual's mental health, physical health, emotional health, social well-being, and/or spiritual well-being. Trauma doesn't discriminate, it can affect anyone, anywhere. The effects of trauma are extensive. The number of individuals affected by trauma cannot be accurately captured. According to the National Council for Behavioral Health, 70% of adults in the

US have experienced some type of traumatic event at least once in their lives. With so many individuals aimlessly navigating life without the proper tools for healing and wholeness, it's no wonder our world looks the way it does today. It's with all this in mind, that I share about trauma experiences I've faced and overcome with the help of God. I believe when we dig deeper, there's always something more beautiful on the other side. Throughout this book, I will excavate as much as I can, with hopes that you will be inspired to do the same.

Will you dig with me?

1

Shame

I had a secret buried so deep. From the exterior, you would never know. I kept this secret within me, believing no one could know. Why was I so silent? Why couldn't I speak up? There are many reasons one may choose silence. Fear of judgment or ridicule, embarrassment, guilt, regret, disappointment, or rejection, to name a few.

Shame to me is that tight feeling you feel in your chest when you've experienced deep disappointment or regret. Dictionary.com defines shame as the painful feeling arising from the consciousness of something dishonorable, improper, ridiculous, etc. done by oneself or another. Shame can also be defined as a regrettable or unfortunate situation or action. One biblical definition states shame is caused by the awareness or public exposure of sin. Sometimes it is related to an injured reputation or sense of embarrassment even if no sin is involved. Another

Hebrew word of shame conveys a sense of total humiliation. With a story like mine, it's no surprise that shame and I became close friends. Shame kept me silent, like hands tightly covering my mouth, nothing was slipping through those cracks.

I didn't realize how much shame I had until later in my adult years as I attempted to talk about past experiences. I realized there was a level of shame that came with talking about what I had been through. Shame for all the things I experienced, which led me into silence for so many years. I don't remember anyone telling me not to say anything, I just knew not to. It wasn't acceptable, appropriate, or common. There were things we just didn't talk about.

My first recollection of experiencing shame was as a young girl, when I was sexually touched by a close family member, and by a neighbor who lived upstairs from me. I was between 9-13 years old. Those experiences were separate from each other. I was first touched by a family member who would fondle me underneath a blanket as I slept. On other occasions, the same individual would come into my bedroom when my door was closed or lights were off. Upon peeking in to see if I was asleep, he would quietly come into my bedroom. He would check again to see if I was asleep before undressing me and himself. He would then attempt to penetrate me, rubbing his penis against my body. He did this more than once. When he would finish, he would act like it never happened. He left my body lying there, sometimes pulling my pants back up. He would place me back on the bed how he found me. There was another time when my upstairs neighbor, who was older, would sit me in his lap as he touched my vagina. I don't remember if I felt shame immediately but I eventually realized those actions were wrong and that I was to keep silent about it, especially the times with my family member.

I eventually confronted my mom, telling her what happened to me. I don't know what led me to break my silence this time. I lived with my mom and my siblings. I grew up being raised by my mom. She was ill-equipped to handle the truth of what I told her. But she believed me. She tried to resolve it within our family. This meant she communicated with my family member and I, and the abuse stopped. We were both kids. We didn't utilize outside help, or therapy. As far as the neighbor, my mom no longer allowed him to be around my sibling and I. We eventually ended up moving.

I never told my dad, we weren't close at the time. I was still too ashamed to talk about it. Growing up, there were times when I wished my dad was more present. I wished he kept his promises. One year I celebrated a birthday at a roller skating rink. I watched the entrance door all night, waiting for him to walk through it. He never did. Over time, this opened the door for a spirit of rejection to come in. I felt unwanted, and unloved. I questioned why he didn't want to be around. I questioned why he would tell me things, but not follow through. It made me wonder what was wrong with me.

As I got older, we started to spend more time together. Out of nowhere it seemed, there was a shift. He came around more. But it was still hard for me to open up. There were times my dad would take me to work with him. I loved those memories, being able to eat whatever I wanted and him surprising me with stuff. Sometimes he would even pay me. I would watch him count up wads of cash from all the sales he made. I didn't mind spending hours with him at a festival, parade, etc., as long as we were together.

I have few memories of my childhood. As a child I grew up on the East Side. I didn't mind it there. One of my favorite pastimes was sleepovers at my nana's house with my cousins. We did girl stuff, like play with dolls, do our hair, and make cookies. According to my mom, I was a good kid. I was energetic, fun, and communicative. I was social-able when I wanted to be. I had friends, went to sleepovers and birthday parties. I had two best friends that I spent a lot of time with. We would watch movies, play games, ride our bikes, and more. As far as school, I always got good grades. I didn't struggle much with school work. Even as a teen, I was mature and grounded for my age. When my mom was going through a dark depression, I became emotionally available to her providing comfort and support. As I got older, I communicated less and less. I became a shell inside of myself. Unknowingly, I built these impenetrable emotional walls. Upon erecting them, it became so hard to come out of them, or to allow anyone in.

Prayer for destroying the spirit of rejection:
"He was despised and rejected -- a man of sorrows, acquainted with deepest grief. We turned our backs on Him and looked the other way. He was despised, and we did not care."
Isaiah 53:3 NLT

God I thank You that Your word is true. Your word says that You care for me, according to 1 Peter 5:7. Help me God to believe Your word above the lies of the enemy. I come into agreement with what Your word says about me. I come out of agreement with any voice telling me something contrary to the word of God. I am accepted by God. I am loved. I am chosen. I am enough. No matter who has rejected me, I am fully accepted by Him. I come against the spirit of rejection trying to take root in my heart, and I pray that it would be uprooted now in Jesus name. I pray that regardless of how others treat me, that I will remain free, free from the enemy's attacks against my mind. I cast down arguments and every high thing that exalts itself against the knowledge of God, bringing every thought into captivity to the obedience of Christ (2 Corinthians 10:5). God I thank You for Your great love for me. Though man may reject me, I always have a place in Your kingdom. When my father and my mother forsake me, then the Lord will take care of me (Psalm 27:10).
In Jesus' name, Amen.

2

Self-Harm

"And always, night and day, he was in the mountains and in the tombs, crying out and cutting himself with stones"
Mark 5:5 NKJV

Have you ever cried, and didn't know why? I did this a lot, struggling to express what I was feeling. These crying spells would come over me, oftentimes, randomly. It was like a wave of emotion would flood my consciousness, making me incapable of doing anything else except allowing it to ride.

I eventually turned to cutting. Self-harm, or self-mutilation, is the act of deliberately inflicting pain and damage to one's own body. Self-harm most often refers to cutting, burning, scratching, and other forms of external injury; it can, however, also include internal or emotional harm, such as consuming toxic amounts of alcohol or drugs or deliberately participating in unsafe sex. According to NAMI, those at the most risk for self-harm are people who have experienced trauma, neglect or abuse.

I don't remember the first instrument of choice I used. I just needed something sharp and accessible. I would lock myself in the bathroom or in my bedroom for long periods of time. While cutting, I would cry, either because of the new pain from the cut or because of what I was experiencing internally that led me to this dark place. I couldn't stop.

I needed a way to cope with what I had experienced. It became a form of release, to express what I was feeling on the inside. Cutting was what I turned to. It was private, and seemed harmless at the time, even helpful. It gave me some sort of relief and comfort. It allowed me to temporarily stuff down my emotions and to face whatever situation was at hand. It allowed me to deal with what was hurting me by not allowing it to consume me. I could cut and then go on living my life, doing my school work, cheer-leading, making friends, and more. No one had to know, or see.

I first started to self-harm on my inner arms. Eventually this grew to me cutting on my inner thighs. I cut on my inner thighs because it became harder to hide the scars on my arms, especially as a cheerleader. It was easier to hide when the cuts were on my inner thighs. I didn't want the extra attention or questions that came with others seeing my scars. So, I cut to numb the pain and to escape what I was feeling. Since I couldn't talk about it, I cut. Cutting became my first addiction.

An addiction is defined as a strong inclination to do, use, or indulge in something repeatedly. It's also defined as a compulsive, chronic, physiological or psychological need for a habit-forming substance, behavior, or activity having harmful physical, psychological, or social effects and typically causing well-defined symptoms (such as anxiety, irritability, tremors, or nausea) upon withdrawal or abstinence (Merriam Webster). I started cutting as a young teen until the age of 23 years old. According to Recovery Village, the average age of the first incident of self-harm is 13 years old. This meant I went years trying to hide my scars, and for some years I was able to effectively hide my addiction. My mom eventually saw my scars when I was a teen and as a result I stopped for some time. I then began to cut in places that couldn't be found. She tried to comfort me and help the best way she knew how. It wasn't enough to stop me.

I didn't know I would continue cutting into my 20's. In retrospect, it made sense that I didn't stop because I hadn't healed from what led me to start in the first place. So here I was in college fighting depressive thoughts, when this old habit tried to remind me of the relief it once brought me. I gave in, which led to me cutting on my stomach. As I got older, the cutting minimized as I found more acceptable means of coping.

My final time cutting was after the dissolution of my first marriage. That cut left the biggest scar. When I saw how bad it was, I told myself I wouldn't ever cut again. It wouldn't stop bleeding, and that scared me. I had moved back to my home state (Rhode Island) after having relocated to Texas. I was married to a woman. I'll get into this more in Chapter Four. Upon returning home, I was in a dark place. I tried to avoid the feelings I felt, which led to me cutting.

My friend named shame returned again. I felt ashamed for having gotten married without seeking the counsel of others. Shame for my marriage failing, and having to move back to my home state to rebuild all over again. I even experienced shame in being married to a woman. I remember being asked about my wedding ring at my church at the time. I lied about it because I couldn't say out loud that I was married to a woman. I couldn't admit it to them then. At that time, I was attending a Pentecostal church. I knew homosexuality wasn't something that was welcomed, accepted, or talked about. So, I kept it to myself.

I kept a lot to myself. I barely told anyone I was getting married. On the day of the wedding ceremony, I called my dad to see if he would come. To my surprise, he did. When I got older, I realized how wrong of me it was to tell my parents last minute, and without asking for their guidance or blessing. But they still showed up, supporting me and standing by my side despite them wanting differently for me. I can only imagine what they must've been experiencing in those moments watching me marry a woman, not knowing what my future would look like. This wasn't my first rodeo though. By now, I had dated numerous women, more than I can count. I first started dating women my sophomore year of high school. My first time seeing an attractive woman was at my all-girls high school. She was masculine so I thought she was a guy. I couldn't deny my attraction to her. That's how it all began. It wasn't long before we became close friends, and my whole world changed. She introduced me to a new world that added to my addictions. An addiction that gripped me for most of my life.

Prayer for overcoming cutting/self-harm:

"Or do you not know that your body is the temple of the Holy Spirit who is in you, whom you have from God, and you are not your own? For you were bought at a price; therefore glorify God in your body and in your spirit, which are God's."
1 Corinthians 6:19-20 NKJV

God help me to stop harming what You call beautiful. You say I am fearfully and wonderfully made (Psalm 139:14), despite any experience or lie that tempts me to believe otherwise. Help me to believe what You say about me, above what I think about me, or what others say about me. May I be transformed by the renewing of my mind (Romans 12:2), that I would no longer do what grieves You, and hurts me. Give me the fruit of self-control to stop cutting, and to turn to You during times when I would normally turn to cutting. I come to You now, believing with You all things are possible (Matthew 19:26)! God there's nothing You can't do! Thank You for helping me to stop. You declare I am free, so from this day forward, I will walk in freedom!

In Jesus' name, Amen!

Prayer for overcoming depression, and suicidal thoughts:
"Through the Lord's mercies we are not consumed, because His compassions fail not. They are new every morning; Great is Your faithfulness."
Lamentations 3:22-23 NKJV

God, I thank You that I don't have to be consumed with thoughts of depression or suicide. I speak peace over my mind right now in the name of Jesus. God may Your peace flood my mind, overwhelming every dark thought that is not of You. I take captive every thought bringing it to the obedience of Christ. I declare that Satan cannot have me! I will LIVE and declare the works of the Lord. Depression and suicide no longer has a hold on me because Christ has set me free, and who the son has set free is free indeed (John 8:36)! God, I thank You for giving me light when the darkness feels great. Your word says that the light always extinguishes darkness and so therefore I won't be consumed (John 1:5). Today and for all of my days, I choose LIFE!
In Jesus' name, Amen!

3

Identity

I grew up surrounded by addiction. Alcoholism and drug addiction were strongholds within my family. Prior to my birth, my parents were drug addicts, and my dad was an alcoholic. My parents experienced child abuse of their own during their upbringing. Growing up, I had numerous family members who also struggled with drug and alcohol addiction. When I was born my parents got clean thanks to the program of NA, Narcotics Anonymous. Through the program and the help of God, my parents were able to maintain their recovery throughout the duration of my life. I never saw my parents addicted to hard drugs or alcohol. I did however observe addictions to cigarettes, material things, and relationships to name a few. Satan tried to attack me in the area of alcoholism too. John 10:10 reads the thief (Satan) does not come except to steal, and to kill, and to destroy. I have come that they may have life, and that they may have it more abundantly.

When I first began college, I started off focused, the same way I graduated high school. For as long as I can remember, I was always an excellent student. School became an escape for me. I was able to escape into my studies, and my books. It was the one thing I had control over, something I could be proud of myself for. I became a perfectionist, striving for high grades, and beating myself up when I didn't measure up. I would have contests with myself, pushing myself to do better than the previous time. This was my mentality throughout my school years.

I graduated high school in great standing, and with 7 awards, the Spirit of Scholarship Award in History and Social Science, English, Science, Mathematics, and World Languages. In addition, I was awarded the Mother Francis Xavier Warde Woman of Courage Award, and the Sister Marcella Shanley Award. I attended a Catholic High School that provided me an amazing education, and prepared me academically for a successful college experience. When visiting my old high school twelve years later, I was able to see my name displayed under "Bay View's Outstanding Women." I'm beyond thankful for every teacher who saw something in me and nominated me for the awards above. I'm also appreciative of the RISE program that provided me the opportunity to attend excellent schools, like my high school. My fourth-grade year was my last experience in public school systems. Through "Rhode Islanders Sponsoring Education" I attended private schooling from 5th grade until my 12th grade year. It was through the RISE program that I was paired with my first official mentor. She gifted me a book on poetry. At the time, I was writing poetry of my own.

Following my rigorous high school education, I went to college ready. I started off studious, staying to myself and in my books. In the evenings and on the weekends, I studied, instead of partying. My roommate probably thought to herself that I was such a nerd. I was. Eventually I began to develop friendships with my peers, and soon after I too was partying and juggling my studies. It was normal for students to juggle studies with partying. I started going out often. Club nights in college were from Thursday through Saturday. I was drinking alcohol, and smoking weed and hookah. In a lapse of judgment, I hooked up with this guy one time. Upon returning to Rhode Island for winter break, I hooked up with another guy I had been seeing prior to leaving for college. It wasn't long after that I discovered I was pregnant. It was my first year of college, and here I was pregnant. I didn't even know who I was pregnant by.

Tightness gripped my chest as I considered my options. I had moved to Greensboro, North Carolina to attend college. I didn't have any family in Greensboro or anywhere nearby. Thoughts I never had to consider before started to race through my mind. How would I finish college with a child? Would I have to drop out? I had decided in my mind that dropping out wasn't an option for me. I didn't see how it was possible to have a child, and complete my education. I couldn't fathom how I would raise a child in a place where I had no family to help. Other thoughts also came to mind, like the embarrassment and shame of not knowing who I was pregnant by. The possible reality of not wanting to be pregnant by someone who I only hooked up with once.

I eventually told my mom. Looking back, I don't know how she felt when I told her the news. I knew she supported me, because when the time came for me to get an abortion she was by my side. She didn't encourage me to get an abortion. It was my decision. It helped to have someone there throughout the process. A process that was new and unfamiliar to me.

At the time, Saturdays were the designated day to get an abortion at Planned Parenthood. I went with my mom by my side one early Saturday morning, hoping to not be seen or recognized by anyone. Upon coming into the area, you're immediately greeted with signs of dead babies along with messages discouraging women from getting an abortion. It was hard to see but it didn't change my mind that day. Maybe if someone had approached me and offered to pray with me, I would've appreciated that more.

We walked in, and to my surprise there were a lot of other women there as well. I felt bad for us. The waiting area felt cold and hopeless. There was no happiness there. When the time came for me to pay, I opted for the inexpensive option since I barely had money as a new college student. The cheaper option meant no anesthesia. No anesthesia meant I would feel more during the procedure. During the procedure I felt uncomfortable and emotional. Afterwards I felt a deep sense of emptiness and sadness that only God could heal. I didn't yet know to turn to Him.

As I sat in the recovery room following the procedure, I regretted getting an abortion. I regretted the actions that led to me being in that position. It was something I never wanted to go through again. That day I felt numbness again, like I felt during times I would cut. I hadn't considered the long-term effects an abortion might have on me. The sadness and emptiness I would feel frequently as a result of what I did. It would take years for me to heal from what I did that day. It would take years for me to forgive myself.

The time came for me to return to my studies, following the procedure. Winter break ended, and I returned back to campus as if nothing happened. As if there wasn't a baby inside of me that was no longer there. The unfortunate convenience of having an abortion is that you can have one, and no one else would know, unless you told them. You could just get rid of "it," and go on living your life.

It wasn't long before I returned to alcohol, my new coping mechanism. There were countless times in college when I was intoxicated, to the point of blacking out. I'd wake up the next day, unable to recall what happened the previous night. At the end of my freshmen year, I returned home for summer break. It was during this time that I got pregnant for a second time. Only this time, I had a miscarriage. I had mixed feelings about it. I was partially relieved. The father was someone I wasn't involved with seriously. It was a situation-ship. I'll get into this more in Chapter Five.

During my four years of college, I was afforded the opportunity to be a part of a scholarship program that opened me to positive outlets and serving opportunities. It wasn't long before I found my niche in the YWCA, Teen Parent Mentor Program. I started off as a volunteer and within a short time became a Project Coordinator. As a Project Coordinator I facilitated weekly opportunities for college students to connect with teen moms, where we would provide mentorship and child care assistance while they attended programming/workshops. I continued serving in this capacity throughout the duration of my college education. At the time I hadn't shared with others about the abortion I had, not wanting to be judged for choosing the "easier route." Being connected with those moms and their little ones had a special significance for me, knowing I should've been one of them. While it helped me in my healing journey, at times it also caused me to feel broken for the decision I made and the child I missed out on. In the midst of pain, and regret, I continued to show up. I gave my all to mentoring, providing childcare, and also overseeing the volunteers under my leadership. Had I kept my baby, at the current age of 31 years old, he/she would've been 12/13 years old. I shudder at the thought of having raised a child in those years of me still growing up. What's most admirable and worth mentioning are the teen mothers I was graced to meet, who made the decision to keep their little ones. Seeing them show up for group sessions while at times juggling a school life, and work schedule is the most honorable feat.

After my miscarriage, I returned to campus to start my sophomore year. I met someone, and he was serious about me. He asked me to be his girlfriend, and initially I was hesitant because he wasn't the only guy I was interested in. I decided to say yes, and we went on to date exclusively for the next two years. Being exclusive with someone was good for me. It calmed me down. We stayed together until my senior year. He eventually cheated, and I followed suit, so I broke it off. Upon our break up, I started to act out again. I was drinking and meeting women. One time I went to Miami with my college roommates to celebrate a birthday. We were in the club. My roommate made a connection with a promoter who supplied us with more drinks than I could handle. He gave me a flower. Somehow, I ended up separated from my roommates, and lost somewhere in Miami. To this day, I still don't recall all that happened that night. My friends eventually found me on an unfamiliar street. Thank God, they found me unharmed and safe!

There was another time when I made it back to my friend's apartment and this guy I liked from years ago was there. We hooked up, but I wasn't completely conscious. I don't remember everything that happened that night. There was another night my friends and I were getting ready to go out, we had been taking shots and my friend introduced me to her female cousin. We flirted and were intimate with one another. We both were under the influence. I barely remember that entire night.

I had a problem. I knew that alcohol had a stronghold on me and that I would need to make some changes, or I would become an alcoholic. After all, substance abuse was prevalent in my family. With the help of God and through developing a relationship with Him, I stopped drinking to the point of blacking out. I knew this was something the Lord was calling me to do, to let alcohol go. To lay it down. A part of me also didn't want the sacrifice my parents made for me to be for nothing. I couldn't continue to play with fire, knowing that it could lead to an addiction I couldn't break. An addiction I saw consume others.

Alcohol wasn't my only problem. The relationships and connections I found myself making were my biggest issue. My boundaries were minimal. I didn't know my worth or value. I didn't realize the importance of establishing limits, because I didn't yet have an awareness of my purpose. I had no sense of identity. So I went from relationship to relationship. I went from dating men to dating women, to dating men, to dating women again. Through it all, I was trying to find something none of them could provide. None of them could fulfill me or satisfy me. None of them could replace the emptiness I felt inside of me. None of them had what I was looking for, because it couldn't be found in a person. I found that uncovering and discovering them never led to the discovery of me. There was only One who could fix me.

"He has made everything beautiful in its time. He also has planted eternity in men's hearts and minds [a divinely implanted sense of a purpose working through the ages which nothing under the sun but

God alone can satisfy], yet so that men cannot find out what God has done from the beginning to the end."
Ecclesiastes 3:11 AMPC

Prayer for those who have had an abortion:
"Children are a gift from the Lord; they are a reward from him"
Psalm 127:3 NLT

God, one of Your commands is that we should not murder. Right now, Lord, I repent for having an abortion. I ask God that You would break any demonic strongholds or covenants that were made as a result of me having an abortion. I come out of agreement with Satan and every form of evil. I pray God that You would heal and restore my womb, taking away any pain that came as a result of an abortion. Forgive me God and help me to forgive myself. I thank You for reminding me of Your love for me in moments when I forget. May the tears I've sown turn to joy again. I thank You for removing all residue and for restoring my soul.
In Jesus' name, Amen.

Prayer for breaking addictions, including alcoholism:
"What sorrow for those who get up early in the morning looking for a drink of alcohol and spend long evenings drinking wine to make themselves flaming drunk"
Isaiah 5:11 NLT

God Your word says You are our Helper. Help me to overcome every stronghold and addiction that has a hold on me. May every chain that has been keeping me in bondage be broken now in the name of Jesus. I speak freedom and life over myself, that I would no longer choose death and bondage, but freedom and life. May I be free from anything keeping me from You! I pray God that You would change my taste buds, change what I desire, change me so that I'll no longer crave what is harmful to me. I will not desire Egypt, those things that separate me from Your presence. I declare that Satan cannot have me, for he is already defeated. Jesus, I'm yours!

In Jesus' name, Amen.

4

I Kissed a Girl, and I Liked It

There was one addiction I couldn't seem to shake. Addiction is tricky! Just when we think we've overcome one addiction, another one finds its way in. In addressing addiction, I can't fail to mention this one addiction that had the strongest hold on me. From sophomore year of high school around 2006/2007 until 2016 I dated women mostly. I dated/talked to somewhere between 11-15 women. In my lifetime, I had more serious relationships with women than I did men. At some point I considered myself a lesbian, because I believed it was my preference to date a woman rather than a man. I felt more comfortable with women. I had deeper connections with women. I felt safe with women. I felt different with women. Most of my relationships with women were short term, they worked for a time until they didn't anymore. A lot of them were fairly healthy, not abusive or anything like that.

I first noticed my attraction to women while in high school, attending an all-girls school. According to my mom, she remembers me going to her and telling her to get me out of my school at the time, because I was starting to like women. She thought it was a phase that would eventually pass, so she kept me there. Not long after, I was introduced to a world that was new to me and met my first girlfriend. We were introduced through a mutual friend. She was white, with long black hair, and it was obvious she was a stud. In the gay community, to be a stud meant she took on more of a masculine role. She was older than me, but saw some maturity in me. Or maybe she just liked the challenge of "turning out" a straight girl. We were immediately attracted to one another. Our first interaction included us hooking up in a pool. She kissed me, and things escalated. I was mesmerized, her being my first. From that day on, I was different. I had a hard time hiding it.

Upon coming out to my Christian mom, she stood firmly upon her Christian beliefs and reminded me of them. To come out means to come out of the closet, to let others know you don't identify as straight. She advised me to break up with my girlfriend at the time. I didn't stop seeing my girlfriend, I just became sneaky about hiding it from her. This eventually led to me running away with my girlfriend. After a day or so passed I returned home. Upon returning home, my mom and I got into a bad physical altercation which resulted in me calling the police.

It got bad because for the first time I fought back, and she wasn't having that. To my surprise, the police responded and advised me to listen to my mom, that there was nothing wrong with her disciplining me. As time went on, she continued to throw the Word (Holy Bible) at me. In other words, she continued to quote scripture to me. She was a new believer who believed in the power of the Word and prayer. Growing up we had attended Catholic services; it was common in my family background. This Christianity thing, outside of Catholicism, was new for the both of us. Sometime after my coming out, my mom was scheduled to speak at a spiritual retreat (through NA), where she met another female speaker. Something clicked between the two of them and for the next several months they became romantically involved. This surprised my mom and I. We suddenly became immersed in one another's romantic relationships. Looking back, my mom believed this happened so that she wouldn't lose me. She's right. Who knows what our lives would've been like, not having her acceptance during all of those years. After her experience in dating a woman, she became more open to my relationships with women, accepting me for who I was, and even building relationships with the women I dated.

My relationships with women weren't a phase for me. They were real. It became a lifestyle for me. I was going to Pride parades, clubs, and events. I befriended women who identified like me, hanging out with them regularly. I even became a figure on a popular lesbian page on social media. I helped to manage the page with other lesbians. This led to me gaining a lot of followers on social media and meeting a lot of women. I wore memorabilia too, rainbow bracelets, earrings, even a belt. If it was rainbow, I had it. My favorite show to watch was "The L Word." I had every season on DVD. My first girlfriend reminded me of Shane, my favorite actress in the show. I liked women, and I was partly proud of it.

It was at this time when I didn't know how to define myself. I preferred to date women, but wasn't opposed to dating men. I was bi-sexual, although this wasn't to be proud of at the time. To be bi, was seen as inferior. It was better to be a lesbian, to pick a side. No one wanted to be with a woman who liked both, who might possibly leave you for the opposite sex. At times I struggled to find my place within the lesbian community.

In the midst of my vibrant lifestyle, God was slowly but surely getting my attention. I remember sitting in church as a high school student, and hearing a message, with tears streaming down my face but not knowing why. In those days, my nana would give me these books about Jesus for teens. I found myself flipping through the pages and feeling a sense of peace, and curiosity. I also learned about Jesus through my theology classes at high school. God gave me a theology teacher who was a source of light and hope to me during a dark time in my life. It was her teachings and love that demonstrated the love of God to me. She saw me, the real me beyond the exterior. She became a mentor to me, and I became one of her best students. One day she was speaking to my half sister and I, when she told us that one of us would go into law enforcement, and the other into the military. At that time, we weren't even able to articulate our future goals or desires. She saw what we couldn't. She was right too, after high school my sister enrolled in the Navy, and years after college I became a law enforcement officer.

God got my attention even more during my college years. I had been accepted into 8 different colleges throughout the US. It was God who led me to attend college in Greensboro, NC. From my first visit on campus, I knew I was meant to go there, although I didn't yet know why. I had also been accepted into a scholarship program there which opened me up to more opportunities. Through that program I was able to travel to places I wouldn't have thought to travel to. This included me traveling to Guatemala and staying there for one month during the summer time, doing service work. I was also able to volunteer at various organizations, therefore building community relationships and experience that would prove beneficial in years to come.

In my junior year of college, two years after I had an abortion, things began to change for me. Around this time, I had started attending a Sexual Assault Support Group on campus. I tried to keep it private about me attending, I still wasn't comfortable sharing about the sexual abuse I had experienced by a family member.

One day before going into the cafe, I bumped into an older woman in the bathroom and she complimented my hair which led to us talking and exchanging numbers. Turns out she was a minister through Intervarsity Christian Fellowship. Intervarsity is a campus ministry that essentially brings Jesus to college students in a real and effective way. Through the minister I met in the bathroom, she connected me to another Intervarsity leader and it wasn't long before I was participating in events and bible studies. Instead of sitting with my friends for meals, I would join Intervarsity's lunch bible discussions. There was this one time I met with a leader in the grill for bible study. The grill was an alternative option to the café, they served smoothies and wraps among other food items made to order. I felt slightly embarrassed. It was like we were in this public place studying the Word of God and I was embarrassed for my peers to see me. My leader appeared to be unashamed, so I followed his lead. Eventually I didn't care what others saw or thought. That day we read the story about the Prodigal son.

As I kept receiving emails about different events, I continued showing up. At the time I was also a Resident Advisor on campus, so I was forwarding emails to the students in my dorm about Intervarsity events. I didn't know it at the time but God was calling me to himself. I had only been involved with Intervarsity for three months before being invited to attend Rockbridge (College Bible Camp). It was May 6, 2012 when I went. I didn't know anyone, but that didn't stop me from going. I returned back to campus on May 11, 2012, only I wasn't the same person.

To put it simply, Rockbridge was a 6-day camp where one would learn more about Jesus, through prayer times, small groups, scripture study, and personal retreat. In addition, there was training and times of unforgettable worship. Beforehand, we were advised to choose our individual "track" or focus for the 6 days. Out of the multiple tracks that were provided, I chose "Connecting to God." A typical day consisted of 8:30am Breakfast, 9:15am Soaking Prayer which included Centering Prayer and 1 Samuel 3 Manuscript Bible Study, 12:30pm Lunch, 1:30pm Free Time, 5:30pm Dinner, 6:45pm 1 Samuel 8 Lectio Divina, 8:40pm Small Groups, 9:30pm Large Group Worship, 10:30pm Free Time, 1am LOAQ Lights Out after Questions. The goal of Soaking Prayer was to just spend time with God, to rest in His presence, and to listen for His voice. Centering Prayer was similar, we sat in the presence of God and gave Him our undivided love and attention. A typical day also included "Lectio Divina," which is basically devotional reading, requiring an open, reflective, listening posture alert to the voice of God. This type of reading is aimed more at growing a relationship with God rather than gathering information about God.

It was through the entirety of my Rockbridge experience that I had a radical encounter with God, and my life was forever changed. During corporate worship, I remember lifting my hands and worshiping to songs like "Give Me Faith," "Forever Reign," and "10,000 Reasons." Initially I was fearful to lift my hands and to worship publicly. I observed other students boldly worshiping God. As the days passed, I couldn't contain myself anymore. I was finally free to worship this God who showed up in a real and personal way. The songs spoke to me. I'll never forget these words:

"Oh, I'm running to Your arms

I'm running to Your arms
The riches of Your love
Will always be enough
Nothing compares to Your embrace
Light of the world forever reign"

It was like God himself was telling me that He was chasing after me, and I too was telling Him that I was chasing after Him. "My heart will sing, no other name, Jesus." These words were being etched into my heart, and soon it would become true. I would sing no other name but the name of Jesus. After Rockbridge I returned home, but I was different. If I could've stayed at Rockbridge forever, I would have. But it was time to face the real world. Before things got better, they got worse. I went on to graduate college in 2013. I graduated on time, and a point shy of making the Dean's List. Making the Dean's List was a personal goal I had managed to achieve more than once.

Two years later, an ex-boyfriend from college was killed. We had been together for almost two years during my time in college. He was someone I saw myself marrying. I was confused by his death, confused why God would allow the only man I considered marrying to die. When I got the news, I was in Tennessee, with a girl I was interested in at the time. Tears streamed down my eyes after receiving the phone call that he didn't make it.

Six months later I was baptized at the church my mom took me to as a teen. I was 23 years old at the time, it was July 31st,

2014. I didn't fully understand the significance of baptism at the time but it seemed like the next step one was supposed to take. Less than a month later, on August 21st, 2014, I was married to a woman. In my own deception at the time, I had reasoned to myself that it was better to be married to a woman than dating a woman. I thought God would be accepting of it if we were married.

In the midst of me being married to a woman, I got involved at my church. I reached out to the dance leader to express my interest. By early 2015 I performed my first solo as a dance minister to a song titled "To Be Like You." I was able to choose my own song selection. "To Be Like You," spoke to me most of all. Some of the words were "Here I'll bow, give all to You. Lord, I want to be like You. All I want, all I need, more of You, less of me. Take this life. Lord, it's Yours. Have my heart, have it all." I didn't fully understand the words at the time, but God knew.

So back to the woman I married. We were both young, taking a risk at love. I was 23 years old, and she was 19 years old. We met through social media. It was long distance; she was from Texas. It didn't take long for our relationship to escalate, and for her to propose. We told each other we were done playing games and were looking for the real thing. We thought we found it in each other. Initially I was hesitant about accepting her proposal, knowing she was younger than me. She had also shown me on multiple occasions that she was still immature, but we both believed in God so I thought to myself, at least we had that.

When I accepted her proposal I wasn't in love at the time. I thought to myself I could grow to love her. I never did. Our wedding ceremony wasn't anything special. We were married in a gazebo at a park, with a few of my family members present. We found an officiant online who was affordable and available. We found her almost one week before our wedding. She advised us we needed two witnesses present, so my mom, dad, and aunt came. My fiancé didn't even tell her parents about the wedding beforehand. We were legally married in Rhode Island, since it wasn't legal in Texas at the time. The officiant didn't know much about us. She provided the vows, and we followed her lead. There was no rehearsal or anything like that. Our ceremony was less than 10 minutes long. We kissed, took our pictures, and left. The officiant gave me one piece of advice that day, to tell one another we love each other every single day.

Not long after our wedding ceremony, my wife was sent off to basic training. We communicated via letters; I was officially an army wife. Her training came to an end, and I traveled from Rhode Island to Texas to be with her. While at the airport, I purchased the book "Things I Wish I'd Known Before We Got Married" by Gary Chapman. I don't know if this was a bad sign from the start, or me trying to prepare before the storm. Probably both.

Upon moving in together, it wasn't long before I found out she had slept with another woman. In addition, I had suspicions about her friendship with a married woman. My suspicions proved to be true, it wasn't all in my head. She couldn't be trusted. This led to us physically fighting. Our environment became hostile, and I felt like I was losing my mind. I knew it was bad when I locked myself in the bathroom with a knife. The urge to cut came again and I almost gave in. As I mentioned previously, my former relationships were fairly healthy, not violent. This was new territory for me. In the midst of a chaotic environment, God spoke to me. While being there I penned this letter to myself, as if God were saying it to me:

"My precious daughter, you are worth so much more. The love you give is rare and not everyone can return it or know what to do with it. So, you must be careful who you give this love to. You have these qualities that are both admirable and a burden at times. You give too many chances, you seek to understand others at their core regardless of the circumstances, you give forgiveness freely, you give so much, and you deserve to receive just as much, in all aspects, mentally, emotionally, spiritually, intimately, etc. I love you so so much, and I have the very best for you. You will know when it's time. Listen to my voice. Listen to my tugging in your spirit, listen to me guiding you. Nothing good can come out of something I'm not in. My one desire is for you to comprehend the depth, height, and weight of my love for you. When you begin to experience it fully, you'll know what to expect of others."

I wrote this on Thursday April 23rd, 2015., at the age of 23 years old.

Sometime after writing this letter to myself, I booked my flight back to Rhode Island. I decided, along with the convincing of my mom, to return home. I moved to Texas in April 2015, by May 4th 2015 I returned to Rhode Island. The morning of my flight I woke up early before the sunrise, and awaited my Uber ride. My flight was at 6:15am. I moved around quietly as if I was sneaking out, as if my wife would've kept me from leaving or something. But my mind was made up. My ticket was purchased, my bags were packed, and I was determined to return home with the small amount of dignity I had left. I traveled to two states before finally making it back home. From Texas to Georgia to Michigan and then at last, Rhode Island. I don't know who was more relieved when I made it, me or my mom.

Shame again.

Upon returning to Rhode Island, I was flooded with shame and disappointment. Disappointment is defined as sadness or displeasure caused by the non-fulfillment of one's hopes or expectations. What I feared most came true. Failure. My hopes had been crushed. My expectations shattered. It took a while before I was able to express my feelings as a result of the aftermath. I didn't feel criticism, or judgment from others, it was mostly self-inflicted and internal. Pressure I had put on myself, because I knew better. I deserved better. Yet I kept ending up in this position when it came to relationships, hurt.

No one but my mom knew what happened. I was too ashamed to talk about it. I felt public embarrassment and shame for having shown off my marriage to the world just to return to my world, broken and alone. I had posted about our marriage on my social media, and had told others as well. I couldn't think of facing those same people with the news that I failed, it didn't work out.

Instead of facing my feelings, I did what I was used to doing. I tried to numb how I felt. My solution was to stuff my feelings down, to avoid them. I believed if I didn't acknowledge it long enough, it would go away. I was wrong. What we don't deal with doesn't disappear. It's only hidden, until there's an explosion. I tried to shrug off how I felt, telling myself "I wasn't in love with her anyways." I used that excuse to mask what I really felt inside.

One month later, on June 20th 2015, I attended a Pride Parade in Providence. It started off innocent, I went with my mom. As the night went on, we split up, doing our own thing. That night was like one of my college nights. I blacked out. The last thing I remember from that night was being outside at a block party. I was off to the side, drinking a Hennessy and Coke when I saw a gay guy beside me snorting this white like substance off his hand. He asked me if I wanted some. I figured "hell, why not?" Everything in my life seemed to be going wrong. My marriage had just failed. I was angry with life and with love. Deep down, I was angry with God too. That was the first and last time I went that far. I told myself that would be the last time I allowed someone to bring me that low. I made an internal promise to myself that it would be the last time I allowed someone to take me out of character.

It took months before I was re-acclimated to my former life. I started working again right away. Upon moving back, I didn't immediately jump back into my church routine. I would attend Sunday services with my mom. As long as she went with me, I was able to hide behind her. I didn't have to answer questions or provide explanations about what happened. I was glad to not be alone. One Sunday, an announcement went forth for a secretary position to my pastor at the time. My mom nudged me and encouraged me to go for it. I eventually went along with her suggestion. Towards the latter end of the year I began serving. I started dancing at my church again too. From time to time my wife attempted to make contact, wanting to work on our marriage. It was too late. I knew there was no going back, after I had already left. Especially after God had already spoken to me, telling me He was not in it. We proceeded with the process of getting a divorce. It took months for the divorce to be finalized. It wasn't until January of 2016 that our divorce became final. I was officially free.

If there was one thing I took away from my short term marriage, it was to trust God's voice. Prior to getting married, I had my doubts but I hadn't yet known God's voice for myself. I was still discerning between His voice and my voice. I overrode His voice, thinking it to be mine. All along, He was trying to protect me. By now, I knew to trust His voice. I knew to trust

His leading on the inside of me. I knew to pay attention to it, and to not make the grave mistake of ignoring it.

I eventually started to see a woman from Georgia. She was the last woman I would date. Although I didn't yet know it. This time I was trying to walk in a way that was pleasing to God. She was a Christian. She wasn't someone who claimed to believe in God but acted conversely, she seemed to have a real relationship with Him. While dating her, I had been seeking God about my desires. I was searching for truth. I was genuinely trying to see if I could have a relationship with God and date women. It was during this final relationship that God began to speak to me, where He began to urge me to make a choice between Him or the women I desired. It was as if I could no longer choose both. I chose Him, privately. Now He wanted me to make it public by breaking it off with the girl I was seeing. It was the hardest thing to do. But God helped me to do it. I called out to Him, asking Him to help me. I didn't know how to change; I didn't know how to stop. I couldn't do it without HIM. I did one of the hardest things I ever had to do. I hurt someone to save myself. I hurt her to save me. It was May of 2016, at the age of 24 years old, when I finally surrendered my desires to God and began to trust Him with all of my heart. The song "Withholding Nothing" by William McDowell had been replaying over and over again in my head. I knew what God was calling me to do, to withhold nothing from His grasp. I had given up other things, but this one thing was the only thing I had been holding onto. Here He was asking for the one thing I didn't want to let go of. God led me to that song at just the right time, leading me to not only dance to it, but to apply it to my life.

I'm reminded of a quote that summarizes the decision I made in choosing Jesus, "change happens when the pain of staying the same is greater than the pain of change." Years later in 2020, at the age of 28 years old, I was re-baptized. Only this time it was for me. This time, I didn't get baptized because someone told me to, or because it was expected of me as a believer. This time it was for me, and between me and my Father.

Prayer for those who struggle with homosexuality:
For you formed my inward parts; you knitted me together in my mother's womb. I praise you, for I am fearfully and wonderfully made. Wonderful are your works; my soul knows it very well. My frame was not hidden from you, when I was being made in secret, intricately woven in the depths of the earth.
Psalm 139:13-15 ESV

God, I thank You that You know me! You know me better than I know myself, even the very hairs on my head (Luke 12:7). There's nothing that surprises You about me, including my temptations and the desires I struggle with. God, I bring all of me to You, knowing there's nothing impossible for You! I ask that You would see if there is any wicked or hurtful way in me, and lead me in the way everlasting, according to Your Word in Psalm 139:24. I pray that You would make me to be who You originally intended for me to be. Make me more like You, and less like me. I am Yours and I surrender all of me to You. Have Your way in me Lord. Make me new. Remove any darkness from my life and help me to see clearly. May light and truth come in and replace any darkness, lies, or falsehood. I thank You for Your great love for me, transform me with Your love. I won't run from You, but to You. Here I am God. I trust that Your way is better, Your plans for my life are better.

In Jesus' name, Amen.

5

Situation-ships

In my immaturity, I went from not dating women at all to fornicating with a guy I had known for an extended time. Eventually, the light came on inside of me and I realized this too, wasn't what God wanted for me. He was calling me to himself, and away from all romantic relationships. In rebelliousness and disobedience, I had sex one final time. Only this time was different, because I was different. I had grown spiritually. The guy was someone I had been involved with on and off for the past 7 years.

I first met him one night in a club. I was at a club with my brother, and he had been hitting on me. He was cute, and my brother saw we were both interested. My brother gave him my number. From there it was history. To put it frankly, it was a long-term situation-ship. The situations or people you return to when other relationships fail to work out. It was familiar and so therefore it became comfortable. We had history. We lied to each other, telling each other we loved each other. We were sadly deceived. Our only connection was sex. At times we would talk in a future sense or even about people we were seeing at the time. I struggled to believe him when he would make statements about us having a future. He could've kept those statements to himself, he wasn't fooling anyone. Eventually, I saw right through him.

The final night we hooked up God allowed me to see what I hadn't before. It felt demonic, and it was. I was now a child of God, giving myself to this person who had no reverence for God. I felt it that night. It scared me to think of all the demons I had opened myself to in allowing that sexual exchange between us. I would never do that again. He had no clue that would be the last time he saw me. He didn't know the spiritual journey I was on, and that it was real. Real enough to break a soul tie that had been established through years of deception. It was in December of 2016, at the age of 25 years old, when I made a vow to God to abstain from sex and to wait for my future husband before having sex again.

I'll never forget the way I felt the last time I went to the club. I remember thinking to myself, "Sarita, what are you doing here?" I couldn't enjoy it anymore. I was uncomfortable. Now that I had made this decision to follow Christ, I had no business being in the club. It was Satan's territory. There was no place for God, or a believer there. God finally allowed me to see what I hadn't previously. I saw the degradation in the way women danced, and the way men treated women. What once had a hold on me, no longer did. God was pulling me away from the nightlife I once loved, and the music that had been influencing me.

Prayer for breaking soul ties:
"Now when he had finished speaking to Saul, the soul of Jonathan was knit to the soul of David, and Jonathan loved him as his own soul"
1 Samuel 18:1 NKJV

God, I acknowledge that I only want to be knit to those You desire me to be knit to. Right now, in Jesus' name, I break any ungodly soul tie that has been keeping me in bondage to negative influences. May every chain be broken and destroyed. I declare that I am free from any demonic attachment or connection and that Satan no longer has a hold on me. God help me to forget any memories or to remove any objects that have been maintaining an ungodly soul tie. Thank You for giving me discernment and wisdom so that I will not be entangled again.
In Jesus' name, Amen.

6

It Doesn't Take All That

It was only through the power of God that I was able to abstain from sex from 25 years old to 30 years old. When I initially began my abstinence journey, I never imagined being abstinent for 6 years. Starting off was rough, but I had made up my mind and there was no turning back. To seal the deal, I purchased a purity ring signifying my promise to God. On December 16th, 2016 my ring arrived in the mail. It read "Worth the Wait" followed by the verse Titus 2:11-12. It reads "For the grace of God that brings salvation has appeared to all men, teaching us that, denying ungodliness and worldly lusts, we should live soberly, righteously, and godly in the present age."

Three days after my ring arrived, a new book came in the mail, "Dating with Discernment, How to Avoid Courting with a Counterfeit." I had recently come across an influencer, Kristy Butler Lyles on Instagram. Dating with Discernment is a Christian guidebook that exposes "counterfeits" that are often strategically placed in our romantic paths to deceive and derail us from the destiny of love God truly has in store for our lives. It also sheds light on the difference between being spiritually led versus romantically driven. That single book was everything I needed during my years of singleness and abstinence. It was a game changer for me.

Reading "Dating with Discernment" revolutionized the way I saw dating and marriage. I could no longer date the same. I could no longer go into relationships without discernment and without God. I knew it would inevitably fail without Him as the foundation. I couldn't continue in the unhealthy relationship patterns I had practiced. No more jumping from relationship to relationship. I could no longer not seek God about the person I was dating. No longer would I invite sex into a temporary relationship with no hopes of marriage. I could no longer settle! I truly needed a reset in my dating life.

It was during this time I submitted to mentorship, by asking a leader in my church to mentor me. Her name was Sharna. I was inspired by her fire and boldness which led me to ask her. She agreed to mentor me, and became a guide when it came to navigating my spiritual walk, and romantic relationships. In addition to submitting to her mentorship, I began to follow Prophetess Kristy closely and she became a mentor to me as well. I wouldn't be who I am today if it wasn't for the many mentors and godly influences that were strategically placed around me. I want to acknowledge the many spirit-filled women who openly welcomed me into their lives, pouring into me, praying for me, and helping me to see Jesus. A lot of these women were much older than I, they gave freely and sacrificially of their time and resources, and it was not in vain. Upon moving back to Rhode Island (from Texas), it was one of these women, Elder Margie who immediately welcomed me back into church. She didn't ask questions or make me feel bad for what I experienced. She simply welcomed me back, almost as if she knew I was coming back. She clung to me, always talking to me when I was around, and I appreciated her for that. She was sincere, warm, kind, and loving. All of what I needed and desired to be more of.

In February of 2017, I attended the "The Purpose Mate Prep School Conference Series," in New York. Around this time God began to speak to me about sharing my testimony publicly. Days after the conference, my first testimony video was released on YouTube. God had given me a determination to obey Him, and the courage to share about my experiences. During this time, I had begun a new career journey. I started to train to be a Providence Police Officer. God carried me through that entire process bringing me to the completion of training. Upon graduating, I went on to serve in that capacity from 2017-2022. I credit the success of my career to God and the amazing professionals that trained me.

In August of 2017, I met a Christian guy. I was hopeful about him, thinking we could date in a godly way. Dating in a godly way to me meant minimal physical touch, and no sex before marriage. On a date one night, we kissed. From there it was history. Once you develop a practice of kissing someone, it can be hard to stop. Upon opening the door to kissing, it progressed to touching. We eventually stopped seeing each other, for a time. Neither of us heard from God about each other, nor did we want to be tempted by one another. We both prayed and sought God about each other, but neither of us heard from God about marriage with one another. We revisited dating again years later. In the end, it only amounted to friendship.

Throughout my career, I continued to pursue after God by attending conferences, and Christian events. At times, even taking time off to be able to travel to some. Eventually I started to take classes on healing, singleness and waiting, purpose, etc. It was February of 2018 when I registered for my first class, "Forgiving, Forgetting, and Free to be Found." It was during my singleness that I discovered my identity in Christ. As I learned about Him, I discovered myself. I began to believe what He says about me in His word. As I filled myself up with the truths of His word, I became more aware of my worth, value, and purpose. I began to declare His word over me. I made bold declarations that I'm a child of God (1 John 3:2), a new creation (2 Corinthians 5:17), and more. Whatever verse or phrase spoke to my heart, I declared aloud pairing it along with scripture.

At some point during my time of re-commitment to God, He spoke to me about not watching porn anymore. My earliest experience of watching porn came through the situation-ship guy I mentioned earlier. He would show me videos to tell me what he expected of me. He didn't show me videos to improve my sexual experience but to improve my abilities for his own benefit. From then, I would watch from time to time. Eventually I found that when I would watch, the desire would come more frequently. I would watch it more and more. It became an addiction that God wanted me free of. Upon coming to this revelation, I resolved within myself to stop and was determined to do whatever it took to break it once and for all. It was one of those addictions that I would stop for some time until it crept up again. It kept trying to creep up, to consume me. Though I wasn't physically having sex it was a means to crave the appetite I had built for sex. As I went longer stretches without engaging in it, it became easier to keep going.

God was changing me from the inside out, including my desires. I no longer desired the fantasies that came with porn. I wanted the real thing, or not at all. God removed my craving for it and replaced it with holy cravings. I was craving the things of God more than I was the things of the world. Sex, porn, and women no longer had a hold on me as it did in the past. I was free. What also helped me to keep going was seeing how I overcame in other areas. I was no longer bound by cutting, or alcohol. If I could experience freedom in those areas, I knew it was possible for me to be free in every other area.

By 2018 my friend and I started to teach bible study on an online platform. Initially I was resistant, not knowing if I was ready for something like that. After seeking God, we agreed to go forth. My first bible study was titled "Who is this Jesus? The Good Shepherd." From February of 2018 until June of 2019 we went live weekly teaching on various topics, such as, holiness, idolatry, deliverance, and more. In April of 2018, I traveled to New York again for another Christian conference, and then the following month to Boston for a Women's conference. By the end of June, I was at another conference at a church I would join years later. By July of 2018 I turned 27 years old. For my birthday, I went to one of my favorite places, this lake area that I loved to go to. I couldn't think of a better way to spend my birthday, then at my favorite place, with God. That night I made a painting for myself. It was something I had started doing on my birthdays, to commemorate the previous year and the new year ahead. The next day I traveled to Newport, I treated myself to the spa and to lunch. I walked by the water for a bit, and was back home that evening. It was a 27th Birthday well spent. Overall, I was in a great place in my life. Nothing and no one could bring me down. Or so I thought.

Prayer for overcoming sexual sin and pornography:

"I will set no worthless or wicked thing before my eyes. I hate the practice of those who fall away [from the right path]; It will not grasp hold of me. A perverse heart shall depart from me; I will not tolerate evil"

Psalm 101:3-4 AMP

Our Abba Father who is in heaven, I thank You so much for Your will and purpose for my life. I thank You for choosing me to serve

Your kingdom in many ways. As You know Lord, I battle with lust and temptation, and I want to pray scripture over my circumstances to help me overcome them. I declare that I will refuse to look at anything vile and vulgar as Psalm 101:3 says. I will reject perverse ideas and stay away from every evil, as Psalm 101:4 says. Finally, the temptations in my life are no different from what others experience. And You God, are faithful. You said You will not allow the temptation to be more than I can stand. And when I am tempted, You will show me a way out so that I can endure. Lord, help me to be knowledgeable of the exit during the temptation. In Jesus' name, I pray, Amen.

(Written by Bryant Conley)

7

The Fall

"Therefore let the one who thinks he stands firm [immune to temptation, being overconfident and self-righteous], take care that he does not fall [into sin and condemnation]."
1 Corinthians 10:12 AMP

I never saw this day coming. Two years after I made my re-commitment to God, in August 2018, I met a woman. One night while working my 11pm-7am shift, I assisted my partner in responding to a residence for a domestic call. I was a patrol officer. I had just graduated from the police academy one year prior. After receiving direction from my peers, I ended up putting this woman in handcuffs, transporting her to the hospital for her injuries and stayed with her for hours until she was treated. I was kind towards her and tried to guide her in the right direction, she was a few years younger than me. Her and another female had gotten into a physical altercation. Overall, the interaction went smoothly. I took it as an opportunity to provide some light. It wasn't how I planned for the night to go. I hadn't anticipated spending hours interacting with her.

Days later she found me on social media and messaged me to thank me about how I treated her and helped her that night. I responded. After days of conversing, I felt the need to tell her: "I don't want you to misinterpret anything, so I'll be clear. I'm not bisexual or a lesbian, and I don't date women anymore. I only need to express that because you mentioned flirting with me before and I don't want to give you any false hope that there could ever be anything. If you don't want to work out or converse anymore, I understand." To provide context, she previously suggested that we work out together some time. Me thinking it may be harmless, I eventually agreed. She stated she liked to train people. The day came for us to work out. At some point in her training me, she put her hands on my body and a feeling came over me. It was a sensation I hadn't felt in a while. I don't know if she felt it too, but I tried to hide it. The training session was over, but she continued to make contact. She continued to try to spend time with me. She would do things like volunteering to bring me a coffee, or make me a meal. We started to see each other a lot. At this time in my life, I was still trying to navigate helping others and establishing boundaries to protect myself. I hadn't realized my attraction to her. She was beautiful, there was no denying that. I thought we could just remain friends.

Eventually I gave in and was consumed yet again, by a woman. One night she invited me to go for a walk by the water, and that night we kissed. I spent the night over her place one Saturday night. I couldn't bring myself to go to church that Sunday morning. I felt guilty, knowing we had spent the night cuddling and kissing. How did it get this far?

Days later I traveled to a Christian based conference where I met one of the speakers, Sophia Ruffin. I had already purchased my ticket to the conference prior to meeting this mysterious woman who now had my attention. While at the conference, I waited in line for Sophia Ruffin to sign a copy of her book that I had purchased. She wrote "Stay Free," in addition to signing her name.

No one knew just days before I had fallen into the very thing, I thought I was free from. I couldn't share it with anyone. I didn't know how I found myself in this position. What started off innocent (on my part), turned into what I feared. I thought I could be a godly influence to her, instead she was influencing me. I couldn't deny my attraction any longer.

So the conference came to an end, and by then I decided to break it off with her. I had already concluded in my heart that while I enjoyed her company, she wasn't what I wanted after all. What I wanted more than anything else was to please God. What I desired was marriage, marriage with a man. I knew I had fallen into the enemy's trap, but I soon realized I was deceived. I began to think about the reasons I didn't want a relationship with her, or any woman for that matter. I reminded myself of these reasons, when I was tempted to allow my feelings to rule me.

I arrived back home from the conference, and it was her who picked me up from the airport. By this time, I was planning to have a conversation with her to let her know I couldn't continue what we were doing. It wasn't me anymore. When I got in her car, there were flowers on my seat. I didn't pay the flowers any mind. She didn't know what I was planning to tell her. Breaking it off was easier than completely detaching. It took months before I was able to completely detach. It became easier when I took a step back and allowed myself to see the things I didn't like. I was no longer clouded by feelings. I could finally see. I could finally see that she wasn't what I wanted, and that I had hurt her in the process.

I repented, for allowing my flesh to ruin my witness, and for falling in the way that I did. For Christians, witnessing is sharing your personal experience with Jesus. In falling into temptation with her, I tainted my experience of what Jesus had done in my life. My experience with her humbled me, it showed me that none of us are incapable of falling. We are to be careful of pride. We also have to be careful when it comes to witnessing, and what we can or can't handle. At the time, I couldn't handle it. I didn't know I couldn't handle it until that experience.

Breaking free and moving forward from that experience was no easy feat. I believe attending the conference in the midst of my fall was a safeguard for me. The conference helped me to keep things in perspective. I couldn't fall back into what felt comfortable or familiar. God's hand was on me. I was no longer comfortable living in sin, when I had known better. After reading "Gay Girl, Good God" by Jackie Hill Perry, I knew I couldn't go back to that lifestyle again. Later that year I went to a retreat. I received two prophetic words while there. I knew they were from God. It brought me to tears seeing how He could use someone who didn't know me, to speak to me. The first night I fell down to my knees with my hands lifted, giving it all to God. Only God had known the deep hurt and disappointment I felt. I just wanted to be in right relationship with Him again. I knew I would need His help again, to break free permanently.

The following year was my bounce back year. In 2019 I was ready to do whatever it would take to never fall in that way again. It was the year I read the whole bible for the first time. I completed a one year bible plan, and also began the Women's Bible Institute as a student. We started studying the Pentateuch, the first five books of the bible. I continued the Women's Bible Institute up until 2022, when we completed the entire Old Testament. Studying the bible for myself changed me!

The year of 2019 turned out to be a great year for me spiritually. In addition to my personal studies, I attended three conferences that changed the trajectory of my life. I traveled to Atlanta, GA in April of 2019 for a Creative Conference. I received a prophetic word while there that gave me confirmation about my assignment, and future. One month later I was in Boston, MA attending a Women's Conference. And then on my birthday, July 4th I traveled to Oxon Hill, MD for an Entrepreneurial Conference. In October of 2019 I went to another conference in Boston. I had been before, but this time I went all three days, including for 12 hour prayer. I had been to all night prayer before at my church, but this time was different. That night was unforgettable. I had never experienced prayer like that before. It left me hungry. After years of satisfying my flesh, I was finally feeding my spirit, and I couldn't get enough. I wanted more and more!

Some would say it doesn't take "all that," but for me it did. My current pastor says this often. Others may think it doesn't take all that, and maybe that's true for them. As for me, it did take all that. It did take me pursuing God daily. It did take me reading my bible daily, praying daily, and worshiping daily. Oftentimes, I would spend hours worshiping. I would saturate my atmosphere with worship music, listening to worship song after worship song. At times, it took fasting, abstaining from food for a time. It took me fully immersing myself in the things of God, in order to maintain a lifestyle of purity. It took me serving in numerous capacities, and giving all of myself to Him.

It took me cutting things out, and separating myself from things I once engaged in. This looked like me being careful about what I watched, what I listened to, who I spent time with, and how I spent my time. I could no longer just freely watch or listen to whatever I desired. I made the decision to cut out watching movies and shows that had sex scenes or that were too sexual in nature. Since I was practicing abstinence, I didn't want to even entertain the idea of sex. Along with this, I couldn't watch those treasured shows that encouraged a lifestyle of homosexuality. I chose not to watch worldly shows or movies that everyone else was giving their attention to. This included watching scary movies. I could no longer enjoy watching scary movies knowing how real the demonic world is. How could I enjoy evil (through scary movies), when Satan really does roam around seeking to devour (1 Peter 5:8)? I no longer saw scary movies as entertainment. Demons are nothing to play with.

I chose not to listen to worldly music, refusing to fill my spirit with lies or things that didn't line up with God. I was so into astrology in my younger years. At an early age, I had a palm reading book. I would look into the hands of others believing I could read something about their future. I had astrology books too. I just knew the dating one I had would guide me when it came to relationships. Yet none of the advice it provided availed to anything. God said no more! No more could I consult these books, these predictions, that were not of God. The source was not God, it was demonic. God had me throw away these too. It's like God was causing me to reject and hate what He hates, but to draw near and to love what He loves. I used to be praised for my intuition, as if I had psychic abilities or something. The enemy would've loved it if I had pursued that avenue instead. Today I know that it is discernment, and the Lord gave it to me.

With this lifestyle change, to others it looked like I was missing out on a lot. In actuality, I was being hidden and protected.

When my past came knocking on my door, it became easier to not open the door anymore. I was a new person. I was changed, different. I knew what I wanted, and what I wouldn't settle for or fall for anymore.

Year after year after "the fall" I continued growing in my spiritual walk. In 2019 I started leading prayer within a women's platform on social media. I continued leading prayer in this area until 2022. By the end of 2019 I began my journey of therapy with a Christian therapist. I wanted to do all that was within my power to heal from my past and to move forward into the life God called me to. Therapy assisted me in this, giving me the space to finally talk and process my experiences and feelings.

Around this time, I had been serving in numerous capacities at my church. I served as a youth leader, we met with youth monthly providing activities and lessons. On some Sundays I taught Sunday school for the youth. I served in the tech and administration area, which included projecting song lyrics, and sending out emails to members, among other tasks. I was a dance minister, dancing alongside a group of women and also providing solo dance selections. Finally, I served in the capacity of a board member within the board at my church.

It was around 2021 when God began to speak to me about the church I was attending. He was leading me out, and into a new place where I could flourish. I struggled with this transition, in letting go of old connections I had formed. At the same time, I desired more spiritually. The church of my youth served a purpose in my life for a time and a season, but that season had come to an end. Through attending the new church God called me to, a new fire was unleashed in me that would propel me into my future. It was a fire that reinforced my devotion to God. I learned the importance of having a real relationship with Him. I learned that it was okay to be young and on fire for God, and to keep my fire burning continually. It helped to see other young believers around me passionately pursuing and desiring God. It was in this new church that I spoke in my heavenly language for the first time. I had a revelation of the value in praying in a heavenly language, and maintaining a prayer life. I became a prayer warrior. This was the culture of my church, a house of prayer. I was being changed by being in this atmosphere.

My church wasn't only concerned with the supernatural. It cared about the natural too. It didn't shy away from addressing the real topics/dilemmas believers face in the world. During one of its conferences, there were breakout sessions on topics like homosexuality, dating, and more. They kept it real, and that was just what I needed. It's what our world needs more of, churches/leaders that are willing to be real about the real things we all face.

Prayer if you've fallen into sin:
"For we do not have a High Priest who is unable to sympathize and understand our weaknesses and temptations, but One who has been tempted [knowing exactly how it feels to be human] in every respect as we are, yet without [committing any] sin"
Hebrews 4:15 AMP

Lord, I acknowledge that I have sinned and fallen short of Your glory. I repent for my sin that distances me from You. I ask God for Your forgiveness, make me right with You again. God I pray that You would empower me to overcome sin in my life, for Your word says that greater are You, who is in me, than he that is in the world (1 John 4:4). I pray that I would have a revelation of You living on the inside of me, empowering me to do what I can't do by myself. You will help me to do it, no matter what it is, or how big it seems, for You are a present help in times of trouble (Psalm 46:1). I can do all things through Christ who strengthens me (Philippians 4:13). My final prayer God is that You would give me clean hands and a pure heart, according to Psalm 24:4. Thank you Lord.

In Jesus' name, Amen.

8

My Little Ones

In March of 2020, my life was forever changed when my two younger cousins came into my life without warning. It was at this time when their mom/my aunt had fallen into the grips of drug addiction and she could no longer take care of her girls. One night while working as a patrol officer, I drove to where my aunt was staying in order to assist my nana with getting my cousins, since my aunt was no longer fit to care for them. This was a hard night. I was grateful to be able to provide assistance as an officer, but it hurt to see my family like this. It hurt to see my toddler cousin crying as she was separated from her mom. I tried to make the experience as least unpleasant as I possibly could, but I could only do so much. This was just the beginning.

For the next two years, up until I moved from Rhode Island in June of 2022 those girls became one of my greatest joys. A typical day looked like me getting off work at 7am, rushing home to get a 2 yr. old ready, hurrying along the older one (11 yrs. old) to her bus stop, then bringing the youngest to school. Upon coming back home, sometimes I would have devotional time (read my bible/pray) if I wasn't too tired. I would run errands like going to the market, etc., then go to sleep for 5 or so hours. Upon waking up I would sometimes pick up one or both of the little ones from school. We would go back home, and then I would help my older cousin with her homework. Hopefully on a busy day like this my mom would be preparing dinner, or I would be. We would have chill time and dinner. I would say goodnight to the girls and eventually leave for work. Sometimes I would go to work exhausted. At times I was relieved to go to work, to get a break from my new responsibilities. It was good for me to get away so I could come back ready to do it all over again. There were times when work didn't feel like a break due to the calls of that particular night. I grew to accept there would be busy nights and slow ones, to appreciate both. This was the career I had. Despite my home life, I tried my best to show up as the officer I was trained to be. I was trained to be an officer who provided positive encounters with the public, as much as it was in my ability to do so. I didn't want to leave a bad impression with others regarding my service, so I strived to provide quality service.

Initially I struggled with parenting. It was hard to put others before my own selfish desires. My schedule was completely different now, and this took some time for me to adjust to. If I'm honest it took tears, therapy, and Jesus for me to adjust to the new lifestyle of two young girls being in my life full time. A lot of my free time went towards my little ones, preparing meals, doing hair, giving baths, doing schoolwork, and more. There were times I would get overwhelmed. During these times I would try my best to go to God and to give it to Him, depending on Him to help me and to keep me. Over time the girls and I got used to each other and we would have fun together. Some of the times I enjoyed most were our dance sessions, and movie nights. We would act silly, eat popcorn, and just laugh, sometimes for no reason, or at each other. We loved one another. One of our favorite things to do was going out to eat at a restaurant, or to Chick-Fil-A. After years had passed, I began to see how these two special girls changed me, making me into a better person. They matured me, they prepared me for motherhood, and even wifehood. They brought me closer to God, and closer to family, my mom especially. They taught me how to love, and how to show up for others in a real way. They are a crucial part of my story. God wouldn't allow me to write this book without including them in it.

During this time, God brought another special mentor in my life, Marva. I was drawn to her realness and her wisdom, not to mention her sense of humor, and love for God and family. God sent her at just the right time, or as she would say "a ram in the bush." She became a light for me, guiding me when it came to family matters, and preparing me for wifehood. When she initially came into my life, I was single and content. A lot of our time together looked like us meeting early in the morning to go for a jog and chat. This worked best for our schedules. I grew to love these times, and would often leave feeling encouraged and enlightened to keep going, and to keep believing. She's someone I'll never forget. Thank you, Marva, for your example and for your love.

9

Purposeful Pits

"So it came to pass, when Joseph had come to his brothers, that they stripped Joseph of his tunic, the tunic of many colors that was on him. Then they took him and cast him into a pit. And the pit was empty; there was no water in it"
Genesis 37:23-24 NKJV

In the story of Joseph, we see a man who appeared to be deserted by God. Sometimes our pit experiences can make us feel that way, deserted or forgotten by God. Pit experiences are those experiences that bring us pain and confusion, that seem to come out of nowhere, without any purpose but to seemingly destroy us. These experiences cause us to question God, and His goodness towards us. My experiences of sexual abuse, and a failed marriage, among other experiences led me to question Him. I didn't understand why I had to go through those experiences. Yet, throughout the story of Joseph it was said that the Lord was with him. In the same way, though you may feel otherwise, God is with you no matter your pit experience. There are two types of pits we will all experience. The pits of life, and the ultimate pit, the grave. Pit experiences occur for a number of reasons, to humble us, to grow us, to show us ourselves, or to cause us to look to God. They can even occur to bring about discipline. We are to seek God as to why we've experienced what we have. What purpose did that experience serve? At times it can be difficult to find the purpose in it. As a result, the pit can do one of two things: destroy you, making you cynical about life and its experiences, or it can build you, propelling you into a future where you place your hope in God. Joseph didn't allow his pit experiences to destroy him, but to build him. When the opportunity came for him to face his betrayers, who had cast him into a pit, he stood before them with courage, and love. He was able to say these infamous words,

"You intended to harm me, but God intended it all for good. He brought me to this position so I could save the lives of many people"
Genesis 50:20 NLT

Betrayal can be hard, no matter what side it comes from, family especially. Throughout the bible, we see examples of how we are to respond to betrayers, with forgiveness. If you're struggling to forgive someone who hurt you, know that God understands and He will help you to forgive that person. This does not mean He will give you a pass. You have to forgive them, so YOU can be free. When we hold onto unforgiveness, it brings destruction to us and those around us. There is beauty on the other side of forgiveness.

There is beauty in the pit too. It's how you come out of it that's most beautiful to me. Others may say what's equally beautiful is your response during the pit. How would God find you in the midst of that storm? Would He find you worrying, and in bitterness, or trusting Him, and rejoicing? How have others observed you while experiencing that pit? Would they be able to say you didn't complain at all, or that you whined every chance you got? Maybe you didn't respond too well that first time around. But now that you know, you can try again when the next storm comes. You can say that you were found trusting Him.

What did you do when you got to the other side of it? You have to do something with it. The goal isn't to simply make it out. We do ourselves and others a disservice when we keep our experiences and lessons to ourselves. It's what you do with the experience that matters most of all. Will you use it to bring encouragement and light to others? Or will you allow it to break you, causing you to turn away from God and others? Perhaps you're not the only one who experienced THAT pit. Perhaps you experienced it so you can share with others how you came out of it.

"And we know [with great confidence] that God [who is deeply concerned about us] causes all things to work together [as a plan] for

good for those who love God, to those who are called according to His plan and purpose"
Romans 8:28 AMP

Prayer to forgive those who have hurt you:

"Therefore I say to you, whatever things you ask when you pray, believe that you receive them, and you will have them. And whenever you stand praying, if you have anything against anyone, forgive him, that your Father in heaven may also forgive you your trespasses. But if you do not forgive, neither will your Father in heaven forgive your trespasses"
Mark 11:24-26 NKJV

God, I pray that You would show me if there is any unforgiveness in my heart. Reveal to me where there may be any anger, or bitterness that I've been harboring towards someone. I thank You for showing me and for Your light illuminating anything hidden from my awareness. I ask that You would help me to forgive those who have wronged me or hurt me. Help me to release others from my grasp, and to give them to You Holy Spirit. I declare I will no longer entertain hatred in my heart. No longer will I allow it to fester, bringing destruction and chaos in my life. I will let them go and I will walk away in peace and freedom from this day forward. I can have peace and freedom because Your word says to never avenge myself, but leave the way open for [God's] wrath; for it is written, vengeance is His, He will repay, says the Lord, according to Romans 12:9. Thank You Jesus for being my helper!

In Jesus' name, Amen.

10

No More Shame

"You are the light of the world. A city set on a hill cannot be hidden. Nor do people light a lamp and put it under a basket, but on a stand, and it gives light to all in the house. In the same way, let your light shine before others, so that they may see your good works and give glory to your Father who is in heaven."
Matthew 5:14-16 NKJV

God first told me to write this book in 2017. Towards the end of 2017, I started to write. In the following year I continued writing. After "the fall," I stopped writing for some time. The enemy got in my head. He convinced me I wasn't worthy to write, and I believed him. I allowed the voices of the enemy, and fear to stop me. I believed the lie that what I had to say wasn't valuable. I questioned the Lord, and asked Him to use someone else instead. I feared what others would think. I feared the opinions of man, rather than obeying God. I allowed myself to be muzzled until God spoke it to me again.

Years later, in November of 2020 I heard God say to me "I still want you to write that book." Fear briefly came over me as I considered the great task of writing a book. Excitement followed too, excitement that I hadn't missed out on the assignment He gave me years earlier. I struggled to write while raising my two cousins. At times I found myself starting, but never finishing. In the year of 2023, free of parenting responsibilities, I picked it up again. He put me in remembrance of it and empowered me to do it. This time I felt a supernatural help and urgency to complete the assignment the Lord had given me. The Lord gracefully brought all that I've shared to my remembrance. He has shown up time and time again while writing, guiding me every step of the way. What initially seemed so daunting became possible with Him. After all, with Him all things are possible. I'm thankful for all the Lord has led me to share. I know it wasn't by accident nor coincidence. Even the parts I didn't initially plan to share on, I do so in obedience to Him. It's with this in mind that I present to you my story, including the ups and downs, with hopes that it will cause you to have your own encounter with God.

It may be hard to believe someone like me could experience so much in such a short time. This is why we can't judge a person by their appearance. We can never know the private battles or experiences one has faced. Look at what the Lord has done! He's redeemed my story. It's only because of Him that I've made it this far. It's only because of Him that I've endured what I have, and am a better person for it. Only God could do something like this. He's kind. He's good. And He's so real. I would love for you to know Him for yourself if you don't already. He desires to have a personal relationship with you!

No matter what you've experienced or the shame you feel, the Lord is able to free you. Before the Lord can take away your shame, He wants you to remember where it came from. In your remembrance, you can finally see your need for Him. Only the Lord can rescue you from deep pain and shame. When the weight of shame feels so heavy, it takes the love of God to erase all traces of it. In Micah 7:19 it says "He will again have compassion on us; He will subdue and tread underfoot our iniquities. You will cast all our sins into the depths of the sea."

I'm reminded of the Samaritan woman who had an encounter with Jesus that forever changed her. This is what a true encounter with Jesus is meant to do, change us, so that we can never be the same. During this encounter Jesus broke all societal barriers to have a conversation with an outcast, someone who was despised and rejected by others. Jesus knew what it felt like to be rejected. Jesus demonstrated that she was worth talking to, that she was valuable despite how others treated her. Jesus showed her that He saw her. He didn't see what others saw; He saw the real her. Jesus' love for her outweighed all her shame. Even now, Jesus' love for you outweighs all your shame. He wants to have a relationship with you, no matter the shame of your past or present. He sees you, and He has compassion for you. The compassion He has for you means "to love from the womb." The love He has for you is like the love a Father has for His child. He loved you from the beginning and His love towards you never runs out, or fails. It's beyond understanding or description. It's incomparable to the love of an earthly parent. Incomparable to any other love. You'll never know a love like His. It's far greater, and better. My final prayer is that your heart would be open to Him. Watch what He does with your story. He will complete the work He began in you, and make it more beautiful than you ever thought possible!

> *"Do not fear, for you will not be ashamed; neither be disgraced, for you will not be put to shame; For you will forget the shame of your youth, and will not remember the reproach of your widowhood anymore. For your Maker is your husband, the Lord of hosts is His name; and your Redeemer is the Holy One of Israel; He is called the God of the whole earth."*
> Isaiah 54:4-5 NKJV

A prayer to invite Jesus into your heart:
God, I confess that I am a sinner in need of You. Forgive me for all of my sin. I believe that You sent Jesus to die for my sins so that I would have new life. Today, I invite You into my heart. Holy Spirit come into my heart and do the impossible in my life. Help me to walk in Your ways and to live for You. I acknowledge that as of now it is no longer I who live, but Christ lives in me; and the life which I now

live in the flesh I live by faith in the Son of God, who loved me and gave Himself for me, according to Galatians 2:20.

I pray all of this in Jesus' name, Amen.

If you want to recommit your life to Jesus, there's no condemnation!

You can pray this prayer:

Jesus I'm sorry for how I've strayed from You. Your word says that all of us are like sheep that have strayed, and I admit I have strayed from Your ways (Isaiah 53:6). I want to return to You with all of my heart. I want to love You with all of my heart, and with all of my soul, and with all my mind, according to Matthew 22:37. I invite You to show me how to live for You. I will take my covenant with You seriously, reading Your Word, and seeking Your face daily, maintaining a relationship with You with each new day. Thank you for giving me the power to do what pleases You (Philippians 2:13). I'm returning to You! I thank You that when a lost son or daughter returns to You, You rejoice. You're rejoicing over me right now, therefore I can rejoice too.

In Jesus' name, Amen.

11

Tools to Grow Your Spiritual Walk

If I could leave you with any practical tools, here are the following I would recommend. First, is to get connected to a Bible believing church. Before joining a church, be prayerful and do your research. One way you can do research is by looking up the website of a church, and reading the beliefs listed. No church is perfect! Don't neglect being around a community of believers. We can't grow in isolation. We need brothers and sisters in Christ.

Secondly, get a bible, and study it for yourself! To start, I recommend the Amplified, Amplified Classic or New King James Version translations, as the original King James Version can be difficult to understand initially. It may also be helpful to start with a study bible that can provide further insight for deeper study. The Life Application bible is a great study bible resource. Upon getting your own bible, my encouragement is to read through each book until you've read through it all. Read through the Old Testament and the New Testament, until you've read all 66 books. To begin, start with the gospel of John and then move on to the other gospels Matthew, Mark, and Luke. From there, read Philippians, Ephesians, and Colossians. Before reading, start with prayer by inviting God to illuminate His word to you, and to open the eyes of your understanding as you read. As a believer or even as a nonbeliever, you want to read through the entire bible, for yourself.

A great resource in addition to a physical bible is You Version or the Holy Bible App. As a millennial, having the bible app on my iPhone was a huge game changer for my spiritual walk. Once I got a hold of bible plans, I found myself completing more and more on every topic imaginable. Bible plans are devotional readings on any given topic (Healing, Temptation, Loss, Depression, etc.) that range in frequency. On the topic of "Anger," you might find over 100 bible plan options, ranging from 3 days-weeks. You can also find a one-year bible plan that will guide you through reading the whole bible. This was how I read through the whole bible three times, from 2019 through 2022. From 2013 through 2022, I completed 350 bible plans. This primarily picked up after 2016 when I began to take my walk with God seriously. The best part about the bible app is the ability to access the bible at anytime, anywhere! There are two other great features in the app that I love and use frequently. One feature is the compare tool, with this you can compare multiple translations at once. Another feature is the ability to schedule a verse of the day notification that is automatically sent to you daily. If reading isn't your thing, there is an audio option available for some translations.

Thirdly, develop a prayer schedule. Devote yourself to praying daily, every morning. If you're not sure what to pray for, you can start by praying the Word. Pray what you've read. You can follow some of the prayer examples throughout this book. During your time with God, incorporate worship music. Look up the lyrics and allow the words to speak to you. Fill your spirit with songs about who He is, to supplement what you're reading about Him.

Fourthly, get a mentor, and surround yourself with like-minded people. A mentor should be someone you look up to, someone who can guide you in navigating your spiritual walk. Someone who you may desire to be more like. Surround yourself with people who have a desire to grow and to obey God. Finally, be a lifelong learner! Expose yourself to books, conferences, retreats, etc. that can grow you as a person. A part of this may also include seeking additional help, through counseling. I recommend seeking a Christian therapist, who can provide assistance that a mentor or pastor may not be equipped to handle. In all of the above, be prayerful and seek God. Let Him guide You along the best pathway for your life, Psalm 32:8.

12

Final Acknowledgment

One of the biggest blessings in disguise was the closeness I developed with my parents. Despite my past traumas, I was able to forgive all of those who played a part, and to heal. I wouldn't change my parents or family for the world. My parents have shown me love and acceptance, in their own individual way. They never stopped believing in me, and in God to do what only He could do. They never gave up on me. They kept loving me, despite my mistakes and failures. They are my biggest supporters and heroes. I love them with all of my heart.

13

Book Resources

On Homosexuality:

1. Gay Girl, Good God by Jackie Hill Perry
2. Set Free and Delivered, Strategies and Prayers to Maintain Freedom by Sophia Ruffin
3. Restoring Sexual Identity, Hope for Women Who Struggle with Same-Sex Attraction by Anne Paulk
4. The Diary of an Ex-Homosexual, How to Understand What They Are Not Able to Articulate by Taliah Webb

Additional Resources:

1. Dating with Discernment, How to Avoid Courting with a Counterfeit by Kristy Butler Lyles
2. Lord, Teach Us to Pray by Gideon Thompson

3. When You Pray: Prayers That Get Heaven's Attention by Matthew K Thompson
4. 7 Myths About Singleness by Sam Allberry
5. Relationships, A Mess Worth Making by Timothy S Lane and Paul David Tripp
6. The Body Keeps the Score by Bessel Van Der Kolk
7. Forgiving What You Can't Forget by Lysa TerKeurst
8. The Other Side of Rejection: Healing the Damaged Soul by Joshua P Smith
9. God's Chosen Fast by Arthur Wallis